The Open University

Mathematics and Computing/Technology
An Inter-faculty Second Level Course

MT262 Putting Computer Systems to Work

Block I
Beginnings

Unit 1
The Course and Its Software

Prepared for the Course Team by Bob Margolis

This text forms part of the Open University second-level course MT262 *Putting Computer Systems to Work*, which among other things teaches the use of Borland C^{++}Builder 5 Standard to tackle small programming projects. (Borland C^{++}Builder 5 Standard is copyright © 2000 Borland International (UK) Limited.)

The course software comprises the Borland C^{++}Builder 5 Standard CD-ROM and the MT262 Templates and Libraries CD-ROM, both of which are supplied as part of the course.

This publication forms part of an Open University course. Details of this and other Open University courses can be obtained from the Student Registration and Enquiry Service, The Open University, PO Box 197, Milton Keynes, MK7 6BJ, United Kingdom: tel. +44 (0)870 333 4340, e-mail general-enquiries@open.ac.uk

Alternatively, you may visit the Open University website at http://www.open.ac.uk where you can learn more about the wide range of courses and packs offered at all levels by The Open University.

To purchase a selection of Open University course materials, visit the webshop at www.ouw.co.uk, or contact Open University Worldwide, Michael Young Building, Walton Hall, Milton Keynes, MK7 6AA, United Kingdom, for a brochure: tel. +44 (0)1908 858785, fax +44 (0)1908 858787, e-mail ouwenq@open.ac.uk

The Open University, Walton Hall, Milton Keynes, MK7 6AA.

First published 1999. Second edition 2002.

Edited, designed and typeset by The Open University, using the Open University TEX System.

Printed in the United Kingdom by Martins the Printers, Berwick-upon-Tweed

ISBN 0 7492 4088 1

2.2

Contents

Study guide

This unit describes the aims and objectives of the course, guides you through installing and setting up the course software (detailed below) and introduces the major themes that will run though the rest of the course. It is intended to take 10–12 hours to complete, including some work on the assessment. A recommended study pattern, based on an average overall study time, is as follows.

Material	Study time
Introduction, Section 1 (text)	1 hour
Section 2 (computer)	$2\frac{1}{2}$ hours
Section 3 (computer)	4 hours
Section 4 (text), Section 5 (text)	2 hours

In order to study Sections 2 and 3, you will need access to your computer and you must have available the course software, namely:

the Borland C^{++}Builder 5 CD-ROM;
the MT262 Templates and Libraries CD-ROM.

You may prefer to study Sections 4 and 5 in two short sessions.

It is assumed that you are familiar with standard *Windows* tasks such as

o   selecting menu items;

o   moving and resizing windows;

o   finding and starting programs by using the Start button;

o   closing programs.

The course team uses *Windows* (with a capital 'W') to denote Microsoft's *Windows 98/ME*, *Windows 2000* or later versions, as specified for studying this course.

If you need to refresh your memory on these things, you should do so before starting Section 2.

In addition to the teaching sections, there is an appendix, one part of which is designed to help you with software problems (like windows disappearing from view) that you may encounter. It is suggested that you treat this part of the appendix as a reference item and consult it only when the software does not behave in the way described. To familiarise yourself with the content of the whole appendix should take no more than about 30 minutes.

In-text tasks (in this unit and all others) are of two types:

exercises   and   computer activities.

It is by *doing* these tasks that you will engage with the concepts and techniques being presented, and so master the concepts and develop skills in the techniques. Many of the solutions provided contain valuable comment as well as answers.

Introduction

The course title, *Putting Computer Systems to Work*, indicates that MT262 will involve computer programming since it is through programs that computers are made to do useful tasks. In order to write computer programs efficiently, you will need to develop some skills which are more generally useful. In fact, it would be more accurate to describe MT262 as a course about systematic problem solving. Although the course will tackle only problems whose solutions can usefully use a computer, this systematic approach is also applicable in other situations.

The spelling 'program' is usual in this subject area.

In general terms, the analysis of a problem leads to the design of a method of solution. A method of solution, described in a way that can be carried out by a computer, is often referred to as an **algorithm** for solving the problem. (You should be a little cautious in talking about algorithms with professional programmers, because the term is sometimes used to mean algorithms for a set of common tasks such as searching and sorting information.) In this course, algorithms (the designs for computer-based solutions) will be expressed in a language that can be translated into any one of a number of practical programming languages. The actual computer programs will be written in one of the commonly used languages, called C++.

An example of an algorithm (here calculating the average, or mean, of a set of numbers) is as follows.

1. Add up the numbers.
2. Count how many numbers there are.
3. If the number of numbers is not zero, report that the average is the total divided by the number of numbers.
4. If the number of numbers is zero, report that the question makes no sense.

This algorithm can be translated into a program for use on a computer, and you will be doing this in the course of studying Block I.

Block I is the first of four blocks of course material.

In traditional engineering disciplines, systematic approaches to solving the problems that those disciplines address have been developed and are fairly standardised. The relatively young area of computing has not yet developed such standardised approaches for all its activities, though some do exist. This presents some problems for a course such as MT262. The course team's response was to try to concentrate on general ideas and methods — ones that are applicable to as many problems as possible.

One of the main difficulties that the team faced was the choice of a computer programming language for the practical work in the course. There is no single, ideal computer language for all purposes, but almost all of them have many features and concepts in common. With that in mind, the team selected the language C++, partly because it provides all the facilities that the practical work demands, partly because transferring skills learned using C++ to other languages is fairly straightforward, and partly because of its widespread commercial use.

The language C++ is a development of the earlier C language. It remedies some of the defects of C, and adds a number of very useful features, including objects.

Section 1 of this unit describes the overall structure of the course and the part that Block I plays within it.

Section 2 is a guide to the installation of the two pieces of course software. First, there is the software that you will use for all the computer activities in the course; this is a general-purpose package which is described in more detail later. Secondly, there is the material specific to MT262 practical work. In this section you will also carry out some tests to check that the course software is correctly installed and functioning.

Section 3 is a brief tour of the facilities provided by the course software. You are asked to do some practical work that involves producing and running simple programs, although many of the ideas used in the programs will not be fully explained until later in the course. The aim is to familiarise you with the basic features of the software.

Section 4 discusses the relationship between the hardware and software of a computer system, and the implications that this has for the programmer and the user of programs.

Finally, Section 5 takes a very brief look at the main hardware components of a computer system.

In this course you are being asked to use a highly sophisticated programming environment, and it is quite easy, even for experienced *Windows* users, to do something that has mystifying results. The Appendix is a source of help in such cases; it provides guidance to enable you to navigate from where you find yourself to where it was hoped you would be. The Appendix also lists some of the things that depend on exactly how your computer and your installation of *Windows* have been set up. The wide range of options that *Windows* offers means that some things may not appear exactly as described.

1 The course

This course consists of:
○ 16 units (grouped into four blocks of four units each);
○ Borland C++Builder 5 CD-ROM;
○ MT262 Templates and Libraries CD-ROM;
○ a Handbook, containing comprehensive reference material;
○ 4 Assignments, one for each block;
○ a Specimen Examination Paper and Solutions;
○ a three-hour final written examination;
○ a study calendar;
○ stop press information.

In each of Blocks I–IV, there are *Units 1–4*.

The 16 units contain all the teaching material, including the computer-based work.

The assessment consists of the four Assignments and the final three-hour examination. Local support for the course will be organised by the Regional Centre for the region to which you belong.

The overall objectives for the course are for you to:

o   develop a systematic approach to designing computer-based solutions to problems;

o   translate designs for solutions into computer programs;

o   acquire basic skills in the use of C++ for writing programs;

o   understand those concepts in C++ that are common to all similar programming languages;

o   acquire experience of using a modern programming environment;

o   acquire skills in ensuring that programs actually perform as they are intended to perform.

There are a number of broader aims. These include:

o   developing an understanding of the problems involved in getting a computer system to carry out useful tasks;

o   developing an awareness of some of the different areas to which computer programming is applied;

o   developing an awareness of the different environments in which computer programs run, and the consequences for the programmer;

o   appreciating the relationships between the computer, its software, you as computer programmer, and the person who uses the programs that you write.

Because desktop 'personal' computers or 'laptop' versions of the same thing are so common, it would be easy to believe that most computers in use are of this type. In fact, they form a minority of the computer 'population'. Most computers take the form of small systems buried within domestic appliances, machine tools, measuring instruments and road vehicles. The generic term for such computer systems is **embedded systems**. For example, any reasonably modern video-recorder has between one and three small computer systems controlling various operations, modern cars have (at least) one controlling the engine management system and another for the ABS brake system. Washing machines, sewing machines, TV and radio sets, even the humble toaster, are all quite likely to use small computer systems. All these computers need programs to enable them to do anything useful. Thus computer programming has far wider application than just producing software for users sitting in front of a desktop or laptop system.

A recently developed programming language, *Java*, was originally intended for programming the embedded computer systems in toasters and other similar devices.

Why should computers (in this general sense) have become so all-pervasive? Part of the answer lies in the fact that their behaviour depends on software, and software can be adapted and modified rather more easily than hardware. Often it is possible to add new features to domestic appliances without redesigning the mechanical parts. Also, features that are more difficult to provide in a purely mechanical environment become easy with a computer-based system. A mechanical bicycle speedometer has to be designed for metric *or* imperial units and for a specific wheel size. A computer-based one can switch easily between systems of units by having parts of the internal program doing the appropriate arithmetic, and can have a setup routine to cope with a wide range of wheel sizes.

In excess of 1 million systems were sold in the UK in 1997 incorporated into speedometers for bicycles!

From the point of view of this course, the most common applications of computers are the most difficult to deal with in any detail. For example, the course team could not use the problems that arise in connection with controlling washing machines without devoting several units-worth of material to the control of electric motors and water valves: there is simply too much extra effort involved in using such examples in a course designed for a wide audience.

The course team's strategy is to concentrate on problems that do not need specialist background knowledge. The problem analysis principles and programming techniques used in tackling these problems are as widely applicable as possible. This basic strategy leads to another problem. Any techniques that are really widely applicable have to ignore the fact that you are working within *Windows* and that you are used to using programs which use buttons, menus and other visual devices. (Washing machines do not usually have screens on which to display such things, though they might be easier to use if they did!)

The course team has decided on a compromise. The problem analysis and programming in the early part of the course will be as general as possible and will, to all intents and purposes, ignore the visual features of *Windows*. The latter part, particularly Blocks III and IV, will consider how to program for visual environments such as *Windows*. These ideas will, of necessity, be less generally applicable than the earlier ones.

Another problem arises simply because the course is an Open University course. The problems that you are asked to analyse and write programs to solve have to be suitable for a single programmer working in isolation, because studying is mostly a solitary activity in the Open University. In practice, most software is constructed by teams working together. This course team has deliberately chosen *not* to include group working as part of the course work. This decision means that you lose some of the force of ideas that are needed to make group working successful, but you gain something in flexibility of study pattern.

As in any subject area, team working requires techniques for ensuring that the parts of a project will combine correctly. Emphasis is placed on such techniques in MT262, partly for the reason just given and partly because the same techniques can help to reduce mistakes for a single-programmer project. One of the major principles that will be used is that any programming task beyond the very simple should be broken into smaller sections that can be dealt with and tested independently. The skills that are necessary for this approach are transferable to larger projects involving teams of workers. It is these issues that are partly responsible for the general approach of separating the description of *what* a piece of program code is supposed to do from the code that describes *how* it is actually done.

A third area of difficulty for any course which teaches programming is that there are two widely used and fundamentally different models of programming. In one, the **procedural** model, the program drives the user. The program controls when it will ask for input, when it will provide output and the order in which various things happen. In the second, the **event-driven** model, the user drives the program. Event-driven programs are the type you use within *Windows*. The program sits around doing nothing much until you generate an 'event' by pressing a button, clicking on a menu item or taking some similar action. Thus, in event-driven programs, the user (not the programmer) controls what happens and in what order. Just to complicate matters further, you may well have seen the phrase 'object-oriented programming'. Objects (in the technical sense) are usually associated with event-driven programming but do not have to be. The course team has adopted an approach that follows historical development; the plan is to start with procedural programming and introduce objects and event-driven programming later.

There are programming models other than these two, but their use is less widespread.

You may already have studied other Open University courses dealing with object-oriented programming. If so, a minor warning is in order here. Conceptually, objects are not a terribly involved idea, as you will see in

Block II. However, the details of how objects look to the programmer are actually heavily influenced by the programming language used. Different languages produce slightly different views of objects, so do not be too surprised if this course gives you a slightly different perspective on objects.

Finally, there is a problem that will be mentioned from time to time, but will not be treated in any depth. Many of the smaller examples that are considered could well have their place in programs for embedded systems. An averaging program might be used in a bicycle speedometer system to provide an 'average speed' facility. When writing such a program for your personal computer (PC), the fact that your machine has limited resources (memory, speed, etc.) is of no consequence because the limits are large enough for any likely average that you wish to calculate. For a speedometer, the resource limit might be so small as to mean that one way of coding the program would work, whereas another would not, even though either method was acceptable on a PC. The consideration of such problems will usually be restricted to pointing out that one method of programming a particular task uses resources more efficiently than does another.

Block I introduces the fundamental ideas that the course will discuss. As stated earlier, *this* unit outlines the course aims and objectives, and introduces the course software. *Units 2–4* interleave two types of activity. The first is investigating some problems suitable for a computer-based solution and systematically analysing the problems so that a solution can be *designed*. The second activity is introducing enough of the programming language C^{++} to enable the solution to be turned into a working computer program. This interleaving of general ideas for solving problems and the way of expressing solutions in C^{++} is typical of much of the course. The data (information) and the ways of manipulating it that are discussed in Block I are applicable to almost all areas of application of computers. Any type of computer for which a C or C^{+-} programming system is available can use the ideas and techniques covered in Block I.

Each block consists of four units. References to units in another block include the block label as well as the unit number (e.g. *Unit 2* of Block III); within-block references are by unit number only.

In Block II, more complicated forms of data are considered, and there is a gradual move towards programming techniques that are usable in any C^{++} system, but *not* in a basic C system. The second half of the block introduces objects, which belong to C^{++} but not to C. This block also begins to discuss explicitly concepts that help in breaking up a programming task into smaller pieces.

Block III continues the move towards more specialised techniques. Objects associated with the visual aspects of *Windows* are introduced, as are the ideas of event-driven programming that enable them to be used. The underlying ideas can still be applied to environments other than *Windows*. For example, a large number of computers run with an operating system which is some variant of *Unix*, together with a *Windows*-like interface called *X-Windows*. The Block III concepts apply equally well to programming for *X-Windows*.

The term 'operating system' is explained in Section 4.

Block IV, the last block, looks at examples of programming specifically for the *Windows* environment. This is the most specialised area of the course, although many of the problem analysis methods and coding ideas will be applicable to any visual, event-driven environment.

You will be *writing* programs on your personal computer, and the programs will be *used* (or run) on the same computer. This situation is quite normal for personal computers but not for the computer systems embedded in domestic appliances or vehicles. For such systems, the program is normally written on one computer (often a PC) and run on another. Specialised programming systems exist for such tasks, and often provide the facility to test programs without actually transferring them to a washing machine, or whatever the application is. The programming system provides a simulated washing machine (or toaster, or ...) on which to test the program. For many uses of computer systems, the ability to simulate the eventual use has many benefits, safety and cost-saving being two important ones.

Finally, you should note how this course fits in with other Open University courses in the computing area. There are companion courses which deal with aspects of hardware and embedded systems (in the Faculty of Technology) and with the mathematical ideas that lie behind programming. There are also courses which discuss other programming languages, databases and the problems that are peculiar to large-scale software projects (in the Faculty of Mathematics and Computing). As indicated earlier, each of these courses has a slightly different perspective. Between them, they can give you a rounded view of all the activities that the phrases 'computing' and 'computer programming' encompass.

This course concentrates on C++ and small programming projects.

2 The course software

The design of a method of solution for a problem is important, but it is only half the story. Turning the solution design into a fully working computer program that accurately implements the design is the other half, and that is not a trivial task. In order to do the required practical work — a very important component of this course — you need a way of writing and testing programs; this is provided by the course software. To understand the facilities provided by the course software, it is necessary to think a little about what is involved in writing a computer program.

Originally (and not as long ago as one might think) all programming was done in terms of binary numbers, which represent the instructions actually obeyed by the processor in the computer. This form of programming is referred to as **machine code programming**. Such programs were extremely difficult to read, and hence almost impossible to maintain. Once it was realised that the task of translating from a more readable language to 'machine code' could be done by the computer itself, human-readable programming languages were rapidly developed. They progressed through **assembly code**, which was initially just a symbolic version of machine code in which each statement corresponded to a single machine instruction, to languages such as C, C++ and Pascal, in which each statement may generate many machine instructions. In parallel with the development of such easier-to-use languages came tools to make program writing easier to do.

Such languages are sometimes referred to as 'high-level' languages.

In order to use a modern programming language, you need:

o the facility to write the human-readable form of the program — referred to as the program **source** — which is simply text;

o the facility to translate the program into a form that the machine can obey; this step is referred to as **compiling** the program;

o the facility to test the program, often referred to as the **debugging** stage.

The modern trend is to provide all the necessary facilities in one piece of software, usually called a 'programming environment'. Many such environments are available. The one this course uses is called C^{++}Builder, developed by Borland International, Inc., and is supplied on a CD. It provides:

The choice was made on the grounds outlined earlier.

o an **editor** for producing the program source; this is really a specially tailored word-processing program;

o a **compiler** (translator) to turn the program source into something that the computer can execute;

o a **linker** for incorporating reusable code supplied by other people;

o extensive facilities for testing the program, both as a whole and step by step;

o libraries of code for carrying out common programming tasks;

o a number of other facilities connected with the details for programming for *Windows*.

As well as the programming environment, which is referred to simply as 'Builder', two other forms of software are also supplied (on the MT262 Templates and Libraries CD). The first is a collection of partly-written programs that you will be asked to complete. Such part-programs will enable you to concentrate on the concepts involved in a particular piece of work without worrying about peripheral issues. The second is a library of reusable code that you will make use of in a number of computer activities. Code libraries are discussed later in this unit.

The rest of this section is concerned with installing Builder and the Templates and Libraries software, and setting some options to make the practical work more convenient. There are some problems associated with guiding you through this process. The *Windows* working environment changes subtly from version to version. In addition, you can change almost all aspects of how the environment appears. It is therefore not possible to be sure that the screen pictures that are included in this section correspond exactly to what you will see. (Apart from anything else, they are not in colour.) However, the *general* layout will be as indicated by the pictures. What may well look quite different are things like the contents of title bars of windows and the relative positions of windows when there are several.

Even if you are very experienced in installing software, please at least read through the following material.

One very important feature of *Windows*, over which the course team has no control, is how file names are displayed. File names usually end with a full stop and some characters after the full stop, called the **file extension**. Depending on how your system is set up, the file extension may or may not be displayed. File extensions are usually used to indicate the type, or purpose, of the file. For example, a file called MyLetter.doc is *probably* a Microsoft Word document. Extensions are often not shown for files whose type is 'known' to *Windows*. The course material will always aim to give the complete file name, with extension, but the name may appear in various boxes without its extension.

Other differences are discussed in the Appendix.

2.1 Installing Builder

In this subsection you will need to have your computer running and have started *Windows.* (If necessary, do this now.) If you have any *Windows* programs open, close them now — this includes items such as the Microsoft Office Shortcut Bar.

When you are required to use *Windows* buttons or select menu items, the notational convention illustrated below is used. The instruction

> `Start|Programs|Borland C`$^{++}$`Builder5|C`$^{++}$`Builder5`

means that you should:

o   press the `Start` button;

o   select the `Programs` folder;

o   select the `Borland C`$^{++}$`Builder5` folder from within the `Programs` folder;

o   select the `C`$^{++}$`Builder5` item from within the `Borland C`$^{++}$`Builder5` folder.

Thus, items that appear in `typewriter font` are to be found as labels on *Windows* buttons, in menus or as names of files or folders.

Before carrying out the following instructions for installation, read them through as far as the first diagram. Then return here and carry out the instructions.

Place the C^{++}Builder 5 CD-ROM in your CD-ROM drive. After a short pause, the setup process should start automatically. If it does not, carry out the following steps.

1. Choose `Start|Run`.
2. Type `X:\Install` in the edit box, and then click `OK`. (Replace `X` by the letter of your CD-ROM drive.)

> If the setup process does *not* start automatically, the most likely reason is that there is already a copy of C^{++}Builder 5 installed on your system. See the 'Important advice' box below.

Follow the setup instructions as they appear on screen. At the 'Setup Launcher' window, choose the C^{++}Builder button. Make sure that `Typical` is checked in the 'Setup Type' window. You will be asked about 'MS Office Controls'. If you have MS Office installed, check the box for the version that you have, otherwise accept the default. Please do not alter any of the default options unless you know *exactly* what you are doing and you are prepared to sort out any problems caused by changes that you make. It will be helpful later on if you make a note of the folder in which Builder is installed. (The default folder is `C:\Program Files\Borland\CBuilder5`.)

> A check button can be checked (or unchecked) by clicking once with the mouse pointer on the button.

Important advice

1. Unless you are a very experienced user, you are strongly advised to accept the defaults that the setup program suggests.

2. Even if previously you have bought and installed a version of Builder, you should install the version supplied with the course, after removing the version that is already installed. It will be possible to remove the course version afterwards, if you wish. The reason for this advice is that the course assumes that a particular version ('Standard') has been installed. If the version already installed is earlier than version 5, it is not essential to remove it.

During the installation process, you will be asked a number of questions. Click on the button marked Next, Yes or whatever is necessary to accept the default suggestion being made and allow the process to move to the next step.

Near the end, a 'View Read Me' window will open. Uncheck the 'View Readme' checkbox and click on Next. When the installation process is complete, you will be left with a new window: 'Setup Complete'. Make sure that
Yes, I want to restart my computer now.
is checked, and then click on Finish.

Once your computer has restarted, you should be able to start Builder by choosing

    Start|Programs|Borland C++Builder5|C++Builder5

If this is your first reading of the instructions for installation, now is the point to return to the start of the instructions on page 12.

Check that you *can* start Builder. You should see a screen (over your normal desktop) resembling the diagram below.

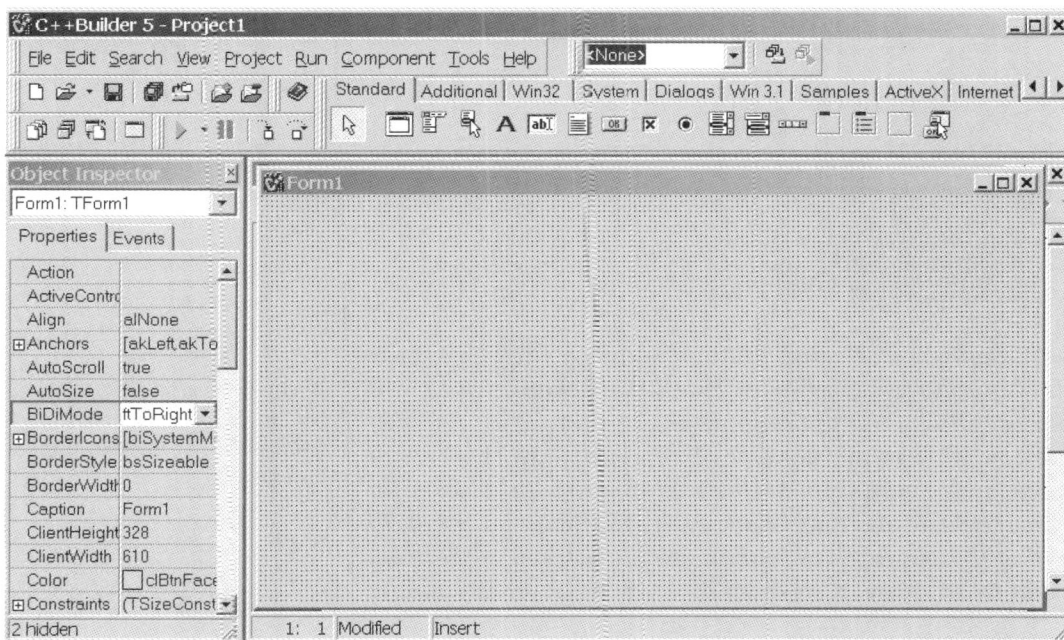

There are three main windows visible:
o   the long horizontal window at the top, which contains the **Builder main menu** and a number of buttons and other gadgets;
o   the window to the left, which is labelled **Object Inspector**;
c   the window in the middle, which bears the title 'Form1'.

If you move the 'Form1' window aside (click on the title bar, hold down and drag), you should see another window: the **Code Editor** window.

The Builder main menu and the Object Inspector windows may have more or fewer entries visible than shown above.

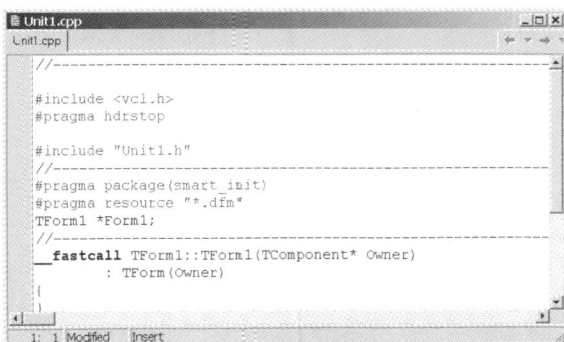

The default state of Builder, as installed, is not quite the best for our purposes, and you are now asked to make some minor changes that will make some programming tasks slightly easier.

From the Builder main menu at the top, select

    `Tools|Environment Options...`

Note that the underlines in `Tools` and `Options` (giving keypress equivalents) are omitted in this instruction. Similar omissions are made in all such cases.

which should result in a dialog box like this one. ('dialog' is the usual spelling in such contexts.)

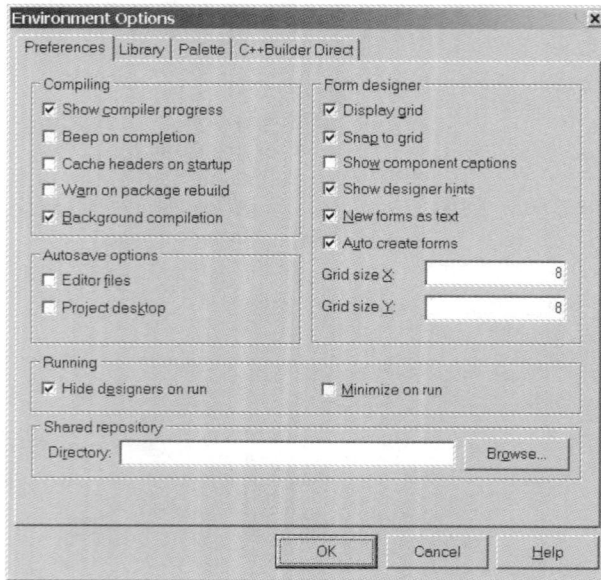

If `Preferences` is not already the selected tab in the dialog box, click on the `Preferences` tab. In the `Compiling` area, check the boxes marked `Show compiler progress`, `Warn on package rebuild` and `Background compilation` (if they are not already checked). In the `Autosave options` area, make sure that both check boxes are checked. In the `Form designer` area, make sure that `Display grid`, `Snap to grid`, `Show designer hints` and `Auto create forms` are all checked. Alter each of the `Grid size X` and `Grid size Y` settings to 4. In the `Running` area, check both boxes.

A check box can be checked (or unchecked) by clicking once with the mouse pointer on the box.

The overall appearance should now be as follows.

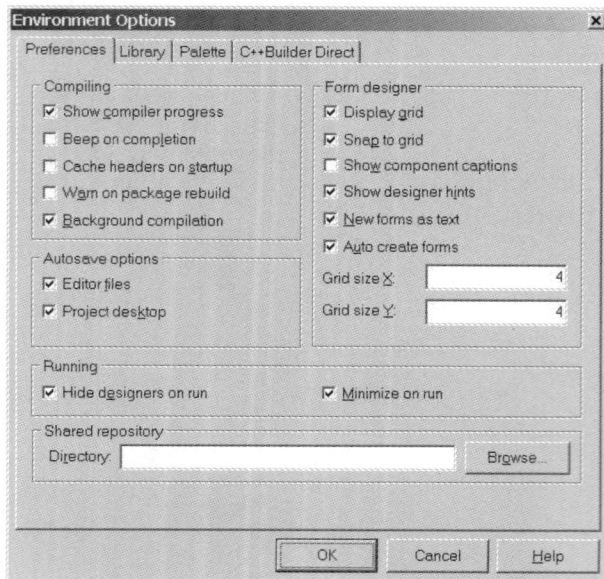

Now select the C^{++} Builder Direct tab and uncheck
Automatically poll Network, click on OK to implement your changes.

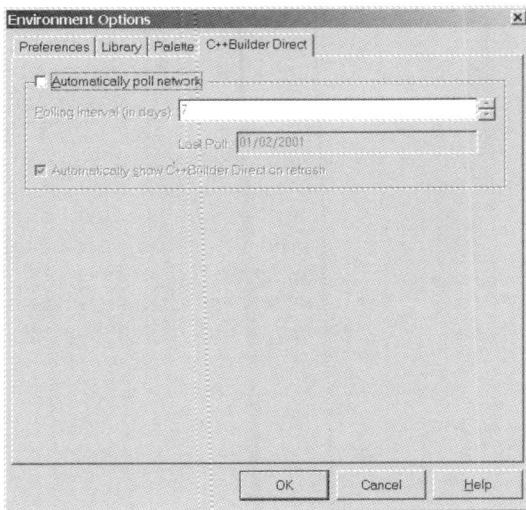

From the Builder main menu, select

Tools|Editor properties...

and select the Colors page, so that the display is as below.

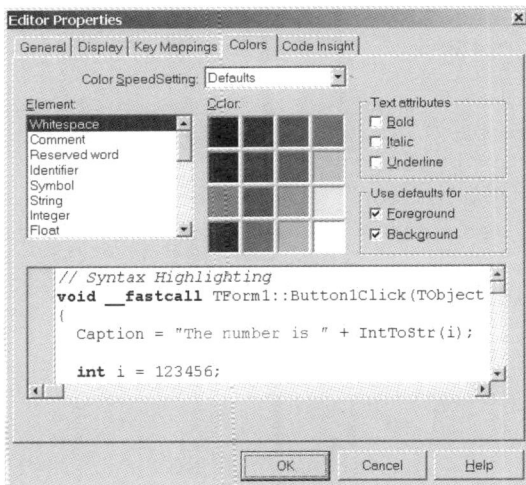

In the Element list box click on String, and in the Color palette click on the red square.

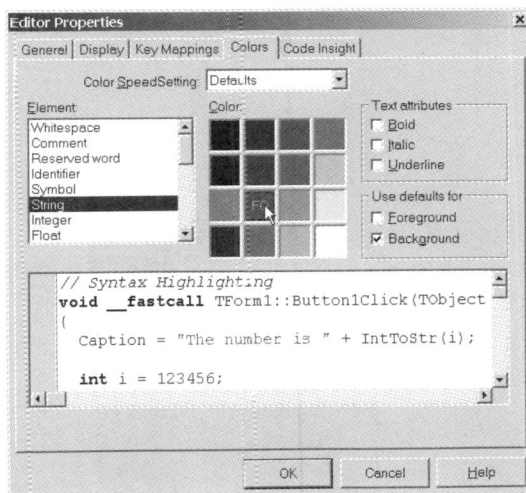

In the **Element** list box click on **Integer**, and in the **Color** palette click on the bright blue square.

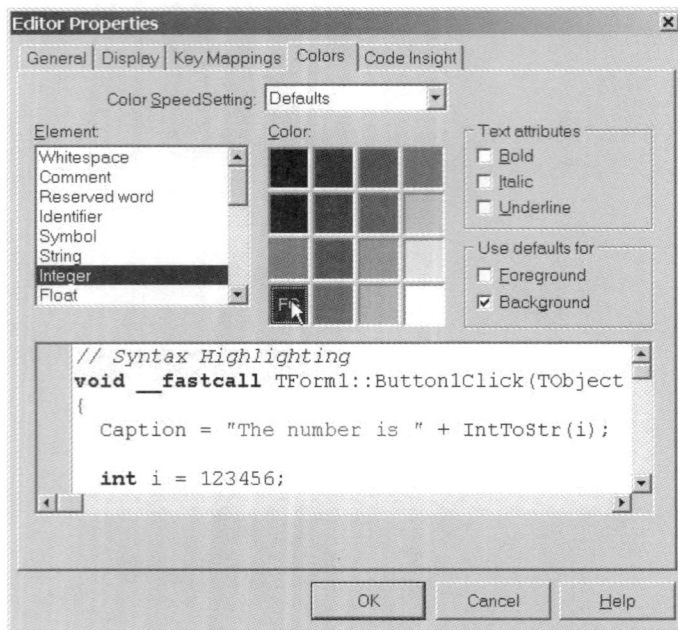

If you have any difficulties with colour vision, you may wish to choose colours other than those that have been suggested. What you need to do is select (for **String** and **Integer**) two items from the colour palette that you can distinguish from the basic black on white of text. If your colour vision does not enable you to do this, it does not matter; the changes suggested are matters of convenience, not necessity.

Finally, click on the **OK** button at the bottom of the dialog box.

The actions that you have just taken will make the editor part of the environment slightly easier to use.

Close Builder by any of the usual methods of closing a *Windows* program, i.e. selecting **File|Exit**, double-clicking on the icon in the top left-hand corner of the window with the file menu, or clicking on the cross in the top right-hand corner of the window with the file menu. You will then be asked whether you wish to save changes to **Project1**. Select **No**.

Do not close the form or the code editor.

Remove the CD-ROM now if you have not already done so.

If you find that you do not have much free space left on your hard disk after installing and using Builder for a time, consult the Appendix for advice on recovering disk space.

2.2   Installing templates and libraries

Place the MT262 Templates and Libraries CD-ROM in your CD-ROM drive. (This contains the templates and libraries for all the blocks.) After a short pause, the setup process should start automatically. If it does not, carry out the following steps.

1.   Choose **Start|Run**.
2.   Type **X:\setup** in the edit box and then click on **OK**. (Replace **X** by the letter of your CD-ROM drive.)

Follow the instructions on screen, accepting the default settings unless you know exactly what you are doing. Again, you may wish to make a note of the name of the folder where the setup program placed the software, *particularly* if you made any changes to the default settings. It is suggested that you always use this folder and the Assignments folder when working on the corresponding Blocks or Assignments.

The default folder is **C:\MT262**. (Some versions of *Windows* display this folder as **MT262**.) The software for each block will be placed (by default) in appropriate subfolders (**Block I**, **Block II**, etc.) of the **MT262** folder.

2.3 Creating a shortcut

It will be convenient for the practical work if you create a *Windows* shortcut on your desktop to enable you to start Builder easily.

The following steps guide you through what is needed. Even if you are familiar with the process of creating a shortcut, you may wish to check the particular settings that the course team will be assuming have been used.

1. Close any programs that you may have running so that your desktop is as uncluttered as possible.

2. Right-click on a blank area of the desktop and choose New|Shortcut from the popup menu. The 'New Shortcut Wizard' will start and ask for information.

3. In the Command line edit box, enter

    "C:\Program Files\Borland\CBuilder5\Bin\bcb.exe"

    if you accepted all the defaults on setup of C⁺⁺Builder. (Otherwise, use the Browse button to find the program file bcb.exe in the Bin subfolder of whichever folder you chose at setup.) Click on Next.

   Use the double quote key.

4. In the Select a name... edit box, enter C++Builder (MT262) and click on Finish.

5. Your desktop should have acquired a new shortcut icon labelled C++Builder (MT262). Right-click on the shortcut and choose Properties from the popup menu. Choose the Shortcut tab in the resulting dialog box. In the Start in edit box, enter "C:\MT262" if you allowed the MT262 Templates and Libraries setup program to use its default folder. Click on OK.

   If you altered the default, you should enter the parent folder of the Block I folder. You should note that Start in does not have any effect in some versions of *Windows*.

The actions that you have taken should ensure that Builder is available easily when you wish to start a practical activity. The changes that you made to the Builder options in Subsection 2.1 ensure (amongst other things) that Builder will restart in exactly the same state as when you closed it down. This means that you can pause in the middle of a long piece of practical work and later return to it where you left off.

2.4 Initial testing

This subsection is intended to provide a quick check that the installation has been successful and that you can work with the program templates that the course team has prepared for Block I.

Start Builder by double-clicking on the shortcut that you created. From the Builder main menu at the top, choose `File|Open Project...`. This should produce a standard *Windows* dialog box for finding and opening files. The `Look in` edit box should show the `MT262` folder name. (Recall that versions of *Windows* vary in whether they permit this folder to be called `MT262` or `Mt262`.) Select the `Block I` subfolder (by double-clicking) and then choose the file `Check.bpr`, either by double-clicking on the name, or single-clicking and then clicking on `Open`. (For the reasons given earlier, the file may be shown as `Check`, without the extension part `.bpr`. The installation process for Builder registered with *Windows* the fact that `.bpr` files are supposed to be Builder project files.)

Please be sure to choose the `Open Project...` menu item, not the `Open...` one. Builder refers to a programming task as a 'project'.

After a little activity from your computer, you should see a display resembling the following.

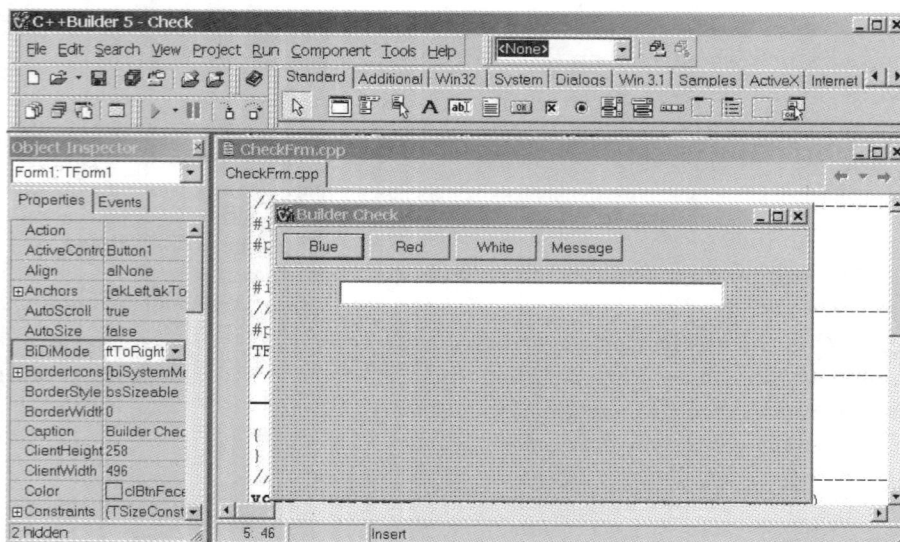

The title of the project that you have just opened appears above the Builder main menu window (in the title bar) as

```
C++Builder 5 - Check
```

From the Builder main menu, select `Run|Run`. This should produce a dialog box labelled `Background compiling` and then, after a short delay, Builder will minimise and the following new window should appear. (You might need to move the window to see it all.)

The options that you set earlier have these effects.

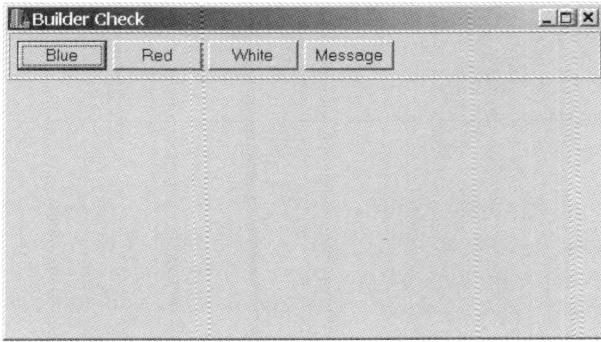

By clicking the buttons, you should be able to change the background
colour of the window to match the button labels. Clicking on the `Message`
button should cause the appearance to change to the following.

You should be able to close the window labelled `Builder Check`,
whereupon Builder itself will reappear. Do this, and then close Builder
(without closing the project). Restart Builder by using the shortcut, and
note that it reopens the project that you were using when it was last closed.

What you have just done is to open program code written (by the course
team) in C++, compile it and then cause your computer to execute (run)
the code. The window with the colour-changing and message-producing
buttons was produced by the code contained in the `Check` project.

If all has gone according to plan, both Builder and the Templates and
Libraries software should be installed correctly. The next stage is to become
familiar with enough of the facilities provided by Builder to carry out the
practical work in the rest of Block I. In addition, in order to get some
feeling for where the course is going, you are asked to carry out some tasks
that will not be fully explained until Blocks III and IV. The reason for
doing so is to give you some idea of the power of the programming toolkit
that you are using. The next section tackles this exploration of Builder.

Close Builder now unless you are going straight to Section 3.

The `Autosave options` that
you set earlier ensure that
this happens.

3 Exploring Builder

The practical activities in this section are intended to allow you to become familiar with the main features of the Builder programming environment. You will also be introduced to a number of terms and tasks connected with writing, compiling and testing programs.

It is not intended that you master these features at this stage. Mastery will come as the course progresses.

A standard 'first exercise' in program writing is to cause a message to appear on the screen and then wait for the user to press a key. You will be asked to write two versions of this program.

If Builder is not already running, start it before beginning the activities below.

It is important to read in full, part by part, the solutions to the computing activities: they contain comment as well as answers.

Computer Activity 3.1 ⸻⸻⸻⸻⸻⸻

This activity does not use the Object Inspector which will go blank.

From the main menu select `File|New...` and, in the resulting 'New Items' dialog box, double-click on the `Console Wizard` icon. In the 'Console Wizard' dialog box, make sure that `Console Application`, `Use VCL` and `C++ Source type` are checked and click on `OK`.

These are the defaults, but check anyway.

The Code Editor window should contain the following lines of code. If necessary, resize the Code Editor window so that you can see all the code. (Some words in the Code Editor are in bold type. This does not show in the text versions of the code shown here. Also, asterisks here are a little lower than they are in the Code Editor.)

```
#include <vcl.h>
#pragma hdrstop

//-----------------------------------
#pragma argsused
int main(int argc, char* argv[])
{
        return 0;
}
```

(a) What is shown in the title bar of Builder itself (the heading at the top of the main menu window)?

It is a good idea to save a new project *immediately* you begin work on it. This ensures that you control what the project is called and where it is saved, and that you do not use the default names and locations supplied by Builder.

The installation of the Templates and Libraries CD-ROM created a folder for each block of the course as subfolders of the MT262 folder. Your practical work for MT262 should be saved in the appropriate block folder. To save this project, do the following.

o   From the Builder main menu, choose File|Save Project As.... (Using File|Save or File|Save As... will *not* have the desired effect.)

o   In the dialog box that appears, check that the Save in box shows MT262. Double-click on Block I in the larger window. If necessary navigate to the correct folder.

o   In the File name box, delete Unit1 and type Hello1U in its place. Click on Save. Then, in the next dialog box, delete Project1 and type Hello1. Then click on Save.

The file extensions may or may not appear in the File name box.

You will always be asked for two names, a 'unit' name and a 'project' name. It is suggested that the 'unit' name has a trailing 'U' and is otherwise the same as the 'project' name.

You should get into the habit of saving a new project in this way (choosing appropriate names) *every* time that you begin one.

(b) What has happened to the title bar of Builder?

(c) Just above the line

```
return 0;
```

edit the contents of the Code Editor window so that it now contains the following. (Use the double quote key, not two single quotes. Read # as 'hash'.) Also make sure that you add the second #include statement.

```
#include <vcl.h>
#include <stdio.h>
#pragma hdrstop

//-------------------------------------
#pragma argsused
int main(int argc, char* argv[])
{
    puts("Hello world.");
    puts("Press Enter to close the program.");
    getchar();
        return 0;
}
```

Choose Run|Run from the Builder menu and observe what happens. (You can achieve the same effect by pressing the green triangle button, located in the top left of the screen. This label is like the one used on audio equipment to denote the 'play' button. The fourteen buttons, including the green triangle, comprise Builder's (default) **Toolbar**. These buttons are often referred to as 'speed buttons'.)

(d) Press Enter, as instructed in the 'Hello1' program window. You will be returned to the Code Editor window. Delete the line

```
getchar();
```

so that you have the following.

```
#include <vcl.h>
#include <stdio.h>
#pragma hdrstop

//-------------------------------------
#pragma argsused
int main(int argc, char* argv[])
{
    puts("Hello world.");
    puts("Press Enter to close the program.");
        return 0;
}
```

What happens if you choose Run|Run (or press the green triangle 'play' button) now?

Computer Activity 3.2

Reinstate the

```
getchar();
```

line, and then experiment with modifying the words inside the quotation marks in the two lines above it and adding more statements of the following form.

```
puts("...");
```

Each time you make a modification, use Run|Run (or the 'play' button) to see the effect of the change. Make sure that you do not omit the semicolon at the end of each puts line.

[*Solutions on page 46*]

Now is the time to look briefly at what happened in Computer Activity 3.1. When you chose Console Application in the 'Console Wizard' dialog box, Builder produced the skeleton necessary for a working program that does nothing except produce a 'DOS box'. (A DOS box is the window that you get if you select

```
    Start|Programs|MS-DOS Prompt
```

In some versions of *Windows*, MS-DOS Prompt is called Command Prompt.)

The lines

```
#include <vcl.h>
#include <stdio.h>
```

tell Builder to incorporate code from libraries supplied by Borland. (All C++ compilers are supplied with a number of standard libraries.)

'Console' is a historical hangover from the idea of an operator's desk (console) from which the computer was given instructions. 'Application' is an alternative name for 'program'.

The line

```
#pragma hdrstop
```

tells Builder how to deal with library files.

The line beginning with // is a **comment**; everything from // to the end of the line is ignored by the compiler. Here the comment is just a dashed line, the purpose of which is to break up the code visually. More generally, comments are used as reminders and for clarifying remarks.

The purpose of the line

```
#pragma argsused
```

is to avoid the production of warning messages relating to argc and * argv[] that occur in the next line. Such warnings are unnecessary at this stage.

The remaining part of the skeleton

```
int main(int argc, char* argv[])
{
        return 0;
}
```

is 'compulsory' code required by the version of C++ being used and by the *Windows* operating system. One of the main advantages of using a modern programming environment is precisely that it provides templates containing 'compulsory' code required by the operating system, leaving the programmer to concentrate on the code required to solve the problem at hand.

The lines that you added

```
puts("Hello world.");
puts("Press Enter to close the program.");
getchar();
```

provide the first examples of output from and input to the computer. The puts(...) statement is short for 'put string'. The 'string' referred to is the collection of characters enclosed in double quotation marks within the round brackets. The effect of the statement, as you saw, is to make the string appear in the program window.

Strings are discussed further in *Units 2* and *3*.

The effect of the

```
getchar();
```

statement is to await input from the user ('get character'). As you saw in your experiments, if this statement is omitted, then when the program reaches the end of its code, the program window closes and you cannot see the output from the program.

Both puts(...) and getchar(...) belong to a code library called stdio, for standard input/output. This code was written by someone else, and neither you nor the course team has access to the source files for that code. What we do have access to is a file that describes *what* the code does, although not how it does it. This description is contained in what is called (in the C++ world) a **header file**. The header file for the stdio library is named stdio.h. The code itself is supplied 'ready compiled'. When the

The #include <stdio.h> statement made this library available.

compiler progress dialog box indicates that 'linking' is taking place, it means (amongst other things) that any necessary code from the libraries is being incorporated in your program.

The header file just mentioned contains a description of how you are supposed to use the facilities provided by the `stdio` library. The description of `puts(...)` is not given here as it uses ideas that must be discussed more fully first.

The following computer activity involves some calculations and introduces one of the libraries supplied by the course team.

For any set of computer activities, you will need Builder running, so start it if necessary.

Computer Activity 3.3

From the Builder main menu choose `File|New...` and double-click on `Console Wizard`, as you did in Computer Activity 3.1. In the resulting dialog box, as before, make sure that `Console Application`, `Use VCL` and `C++` are checked. Click on `OK`. (If there are unsaved changes to what you were working on, you will be prompted to save them.)

The Object Inspector is not used here either so will remain blank.

Next save the project, giving it the name 'VAT', as follows. From the Builder main menu, choose `File|Save Project As...`. In the dialog box that appears, make sure that the `Save in` box shows `MT262`. Double-click on `Block I` in the larger window. In the `File name` box, type in `VATU` in place of `Unit1`, click on `Save` and type in `VAT` in place of `Project1`, and click on `Save`.

Edit the skeleton provided so that the part after the comment line is exactly as follows.

```
#pragma argsused
int main(int argc, char* argv[])
{
float Price;
float VatRate;
float Vat;

  Price = 6.20;
  VatRate = 0.175;
  Vat = Price * VatRate;
  Price = Price + Vat;

  WriteString("Price including VAT is ");
  WriteFloat(Price);

  getchar();
      return 0;
}
```

(a) Attempt to run the program, and make a note of the errors that appear in the new section at the bottom of the Code Editor window.

(b) The errors arising in part (a) occur because `WriteString`, `WriteFloat` and `getchar` are made available through the MT262 course library and there is no `#include` statement to tell the compiler where to find them. Just adding an `#include` statement will not have the desired effect; what is needed is to tell Builder to add the necessary file to the project, so that its internal information about the whole project is brought up to date.

Choose `Project|Add to Project...`, type `MT262io.lib` in the file name box, and then click on `Open`.

The file button in the Toolbar with the green plus sign by it provides a shortcut for this menu choice.

Add the line

```
#include "MT262io.h"
```

just before the

```
#pragma hdrstop
```

line.

Run the revised program. Does it compile and run correctly?

Close the program window by pressing `Enter` when the program is running correctly.

[*Solution on page 47*]

Computer Activity 3.3 did several things. First it described the steps necessary to incorporate the MT262 course library in a project. It is a good idea to get into the habit of adding

```
#include "MT262io.h"
```

to every new console application, and using

```
Project|Add to Project...
```

to add `MT262io.lib` just after saving the project with its correct name. Secondly, it introduced some new C++ terms. The C++ ideas are discussed briefly now.

Your experiment in Computer Activity 3.1 contained some data (information). It was in the form of a **string** of characters which were written to the program window by the `puts(. .)` C++ statement. In Computer Activity 3.3, numerical data was involved as well. The most important new idea in the VAT project is that Builder needs to be told about any piece of data and how you wish to refer to it. The program was intended to calculate the VAT on a particular price (6.20) and then write out the VAT-inclusive price. These calculations could have been done with just the particular price and VAT rate (0.175 is 17.5% as a decimal fraction), without making reference to the items `Price`, `VatRate` and `Vat`. However, that would not have revealed the *method* of calculating such VAT-inclusive prices, nor have illustrated the following points.

The course team is not entirely clear how the term 'string' came to be so widely used for this purpose.

The design for calculating VAT-inclusive prices from VAT-exclusive ones is straightforward.

1   calculate VAT payable
2   add VAT to VAT-exclusive price
3   write out total

So that the program can reflect the above design and could calculate other prices, three *variables* have been used. The C^{++} statements

```cpp
float Price;
float VatRate;
float Vat;
```

say that three data items which are decimal numbers (`float` is C^{++}-speak for such numbers) will be used, and that they will be referred to as `Price`, `VatRate` and `Vat`.

The effect is that Builder knows that three portions of the computer's memory must be reserved for three numbers of that type, and the labels given are to refer to those portions of memory. A visual model is the following: imagine the labels, or *identifiers*, as referring to three wipe-clean boards.

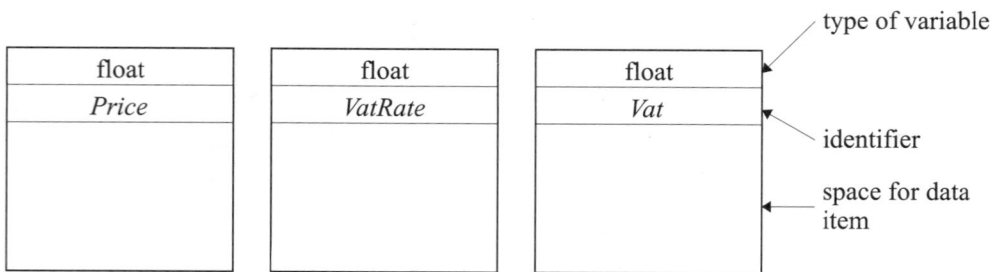

Builder needs to know what type of data is associated with a name so that the code for manipulating the data will be generated correctly. It can also check that you are asking for reasonable things to be done with your data. For example, multiplying two characters together is likely to be a mistake.

The statements

```cpp
Price = 6.20;
VatRate = 0.175;
```

set the values of `Price` and `VatRate`. The '=' sign is *not* comparing values: it is an instruction to write the value on the right on the board carrying the label on the left. Thus the boards have 6.20 and 0.175 written on them. The next line

```cpp
Vat = Price * VatRate;
```

multiplies (*) the value on the `Price` board by the value on the `VatRate` board and writes the result on the `Vat` board. The next line

The * sign is used for multiplication in C^{++} and most other computer languages.

```cpp
Price = Price + Vat;
```

does the calculation on the right and *replaces* the value on the `Price` board with the result. (The original, VAT-exclusive price is lost.)

Areas of memory ('boards') used for holding data items are referred to as **variables**. The labels for variables are examples of **identifiers**. All programming languages have strict rules about the naming of identifiers. Although it is more restrictive than necessary, it is convenient to use only upper- and lower-case letters. It is also good practice to choose illustrative names as far as possible, and where words are run together (as in `VatRate`) to use a capital letter at the start of each word. You should adopt this convention when choosing identifiers for variables. Since variables are data items, nouns will be used as identifiers for them. You have already seen identifiers for actions as well as variables (`puts(...)`, for example); for actions, verbs (or abbreviations for verbs) will be used.

Spaces are forbidden in identifiers in most computer languages.

Variables, identifiers and their use are discussed more fully in the remaining units of this block.

In the next computer activity, you are asked to build a simple *Windows* program, as opposed to the 'console applications' of the previous computer activities. This provides a preview of the sort of work you will be doing in Block III. Do not try to master the details at this stage.

Computer Activity 3.4

This activity uses the Object Inspector; if it is not visible, choose `View|Object Inspector` (or press `F11`) to restore it.

Choose `File|New...`, and this time double-click on the `Application` icon. (If there are unsaved changes to what you were working on, you will be prompted to save them.) Arrange the windows, if necessary, so that you can see (part of each of) the Code Editor window, the window labelled 'Form1', and the Object Inspector window. You will be writing very little in the Code Editor window, so it need not be very large. You will mainly be using the Object Inspector, 'Form1' and Builder's Component Palette, which lies to the right of the Toolbar and has tabs labelled `Standard`, `Additional`, etc., as shown below. (If you position the mouse pointer over an item on Builder's Toolbar and leave it there for a few moments, an indication of the role of that item will appear. You can repeat this action to find out about any item on Builder's Toolbar and Component Palette, but be careful not to click the mouse when inspecting these brief descriptions.)

Choosing `Application` sets up a *Windows* program rather than a console application.

The Code Editor window may be 'completely' hidden by 'Form1'. If so, press `F12`.

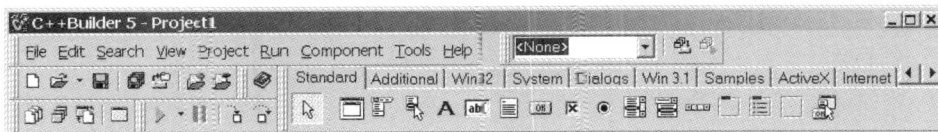

You should now save the new project. Choose

    File|Save Project As...

Make sure that the current folder is `Block I`, and then enter first `HelloFormU` in place of `Unit1` in the `File name` part of the resulting dialog box, click on `Save` and then enter `Hello2` in place of `Project1` and finally click on `Save`.

The current folder is shown in the `Save in` part of the dialog box.

There are more files associated with a *Windows* program than with a console application. Even for the simplest such program, there will be a file containing the code for the program window and one for the project information. There are others, but Builder names them automatically, based on the names you choose for the window code file and the project file.

(a) Make sure that the `Properties` tab is selected in the Object Inspector and click in the left-hand column on the word `Caption`. You can now type into the box in the right-hand column. Type in the word `Hello`. What change occurs to 'Form1'?

(b) Compile and run the program by using `Run|Run` (or the 'play' button). When you have observed what happens, close the resulting window.

Next you are asked to add a button to the program window.

(c) Click on the `Standard` tab on Builder's Component Palette, and then click on the small button icon labelled 'OK'. If you now click somewhere in the window with the 'Hello' caption, you will place a button on that window. What appears in the Object Inspector when you do this?

If the Code Editor window is obscuring the 'Hello' window, press F12.

(d) Use the Object Inspector to change the caption on the button to `Exit` (from 'Button1'). By dragging the button, place it where you wish in the 'Hello' window.

You should save changes to a project regularly. Once the project is named, all you need to do is use `File|Save`. (`Ctrl+S` is a keyboard shortcut for saving.)

Save this project and run it. Does clicking the new button do anything? Close the program window.

Since you have not yet written *any* code (although Builder has created quite a lot behind the scenes), it is not surprising that the `Exit` button does not do anything. You have not yet told your program how to respond to the event of the button being clicked.

(e) (i) Double-click on the `Exit` button in the 'Hello' window. What happens?

(ii) Add the statement `Close();`, as indicated below.

```
void __fastcall TForm1::Button1Click(TObject *Sender)
{
    Close();
}
```

(Please take care that the spelling is exactly correct, with upper- and lower-case letters appearing as indicated.)

Save and then run the new version. Does the button now work?

(iii) Single-click on the `Exit` button in the 'Hello' window, and click on the `Events` tab in the Object Inspector. What do you observe?

If the 'Hello' window is obscured by the Code Editor window, press F12.

[*Solution on page 47*]

Compared with a console application (a procedural program), a *Windows* program has at least one additional design stage. You need to design the visual appearance of your program window(s), button(s), and so on.

Builder refers to program windows as **forms** at the design stage. The program you just worked on has a single window (form) on which you placed a button.

The various visual components (forms, buttons, menus, etc.) have **properties** which you can set or change by using the Object Inspector **Properties** tab. At a minimum, it is usually necessary to change the caption property so that it is clear what the visual device is intended to do.

Property is a technical term in C++Builder programming that will be discussed in Block III.

Once the visual design is complete, you then have to make connections between events (such as a button being clicked) and code to carry out the intended action. This connection may be made by double-clicking on the button (or other device) and filling in the necessary code in a skeleton constructed by Builder.

If you inspect the code (using the Code Editor), you will find that there appears to be very little in the `Hello2` project. However, the compiler progress dialog box shows that several *thousand* lines of code have been compiled and linked. (If you want to see how many, choose `Project|Build Hello2` from the Builder main menu. The program will compile but not run, and you will see the report in the dialog box when it has finished.) Most of the code involved is that for creating windows and buttons, and is contained in various libraries supplied by Borland.

The other thing that you may wish to note is that writing a program (particularly a *Windows* one) causes several files to be created. (You can see these files by using *Windows* Explorer to inspect the contents of the `MT262\Block I` folder.) For example, the first 'Hello world' program involves amongst many others `hello1.bpr`, `hello1U.cpp`, `hello1U.obj` and `hello1.exe`. Of these, the only one that you edited was `hello1U.cpp`, which contained the code for the program. The *Windows* version, `Hello2`, has even more files.

Builder refers to a programming task as a **project**, and the information about the various parts of the project are contained in a **makefile**. This will have the name of the project with extension `bpr`. The makefile for the `Hello1` project was the file `hello1.bpr`. When you open a project, using `File|Open Project...`, it is the makefile that you select in the dialog box. The makefile contents are governed by a fairly complex set of rules, and writing and maintaining makefiles used to be an onerous task for C/C++ programmers. Many of the modern programming environments lessen the burden by creating and updating the makefile automatically. Provided that you use Builder in the way that is intended, you will not need to worry about the contents of the makefile.

The `.bpr` file is the Builder project file. The `.exe` file is the *executable* file that *Windows* loads and runs. The `.obj` files are *object code* files which contain the code for individual parts of a program. When you see the message 'linking...' in Builder, the object files are being combined to make the executable file.

Computer Activity 3.5

If you have the time, it is suggested that you now explore some of the sample programs supplied with Builder. The full default installation will have placed an `Examples` folder in the main `CBuilder5` folder. There are a number of subfolders of `Examples`, each containing a sample program. You can open them by using the `File|Open Project...` menu item on the Builder main menu.

Two of the projects that you might find useful to explore are given below. To find them, first navigate to
`Program Files\Borland\CBuilder5\Examples\Apps`
and then you will find the examples using the paths described below.

(a) `ColorDlg\colordlg.bpr`

(b) `Doodle\doodle.bpr`

Run each project that you explore.

[*Solution on page 47*]

4 Using computers

The broad distinction between embedded computer systems and all other computers has been mentioned earlier. In this section an overview of how each type of computer system is put to use is given, and some of the implications for the programmer are considered.

All computer systems have some features in common, which can be summarised in the following diagram.

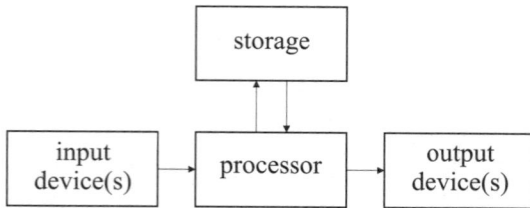

The various parts of this diagram are discussed more fully in the next section. For now just observe that, to do useful work, the system must have some way of being given information, some way of storing and processing that information, and some way of giving (processed) information back to the user.

4.1 Embedded systems

In an embedded system, input can come both from a human user (of whatever appliance the system is embedded in) and from various components of the appliance. Equally, output may go to parts of the appliance or to the user by means of lights or some other sort of display. A bicycle speedometer provides an example; input comes from a sensor every time a wheel rotates, from an internal clock and also from switches that the user can press (e.g. a start/stop button). The bicycle speedometer output appears on a display.

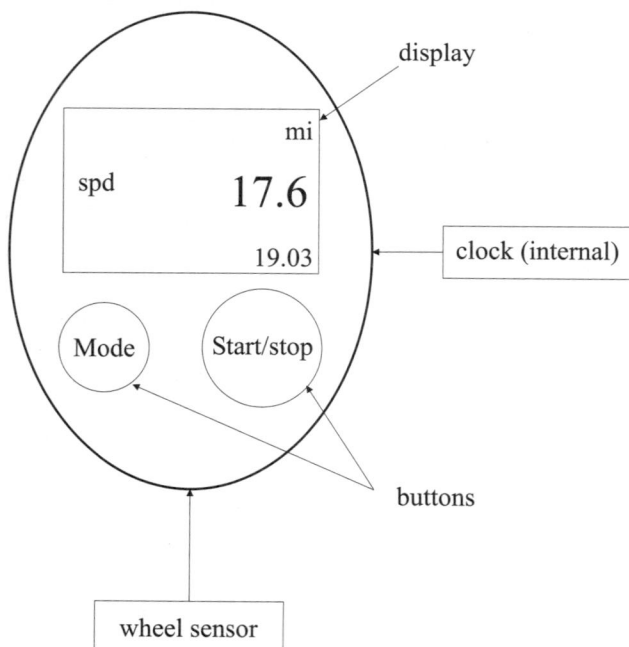

This example has both types of input mentioned above, but only output to the user. A washing machine controller, for example, would have input from the user and from water temperature and water level sensors. It would have output to the user (showing the progress of the wash cycle) and to control the water heater, motor and water valves.

Storage is necessary because information may need to be saved for later use. For example, the speedometer keeps track of how far the bicycle has gone (by counting turns of the wheel) and how long it has taken (by counting clock ticks), so that the average speed can be provided. It also counts (separately) the clock ticks for each turn of the wheel, so that the current speed can be calculated and displayed.

Storage is also needed for the program itself. This may or may not be a portion of the storage used for doing calculations. Some of the relevant issues are discussed in Section 5.

The procedural and event-driven models for programming have been mentioned in Section 1. Programming for embedded systems can take both approaches. For a speedometer, the procedural model would mean that the program continually *asked* the wheel sensor if a turn had been completed, the clock if a tick had happened yet, and the switches if the user had pressed one. The event-driven model would have wheel turns or clock ticks generating events that the system responded to, in the same way that *Windows* responds to keypresses or mouse button clicks. In practice, the hardware used in embedded systems has facilities for either approach, and sometimes a mixture is used.

In the context of embedded systems, this is called a **polling** approach.

In the context of embedded systems, this is referred to as an **interrupt-driven** approach.

A non-computing analogy is of a supervisor of a group of workers. In the procedural (or polling) system, the supervisor continually circulates, checking for progress and problems. In the event-driven (or interrupt-driven) system, the supervisor waits for a worker to request attention. Both approaches have benefits and snags. Polling has the computer system (supervisor) firmly in charge, but a critical problem or event may occur just after the supervisor has visited, and will not be dealt with until the next visit. Sometimes such delays could cause a disaster. On the other hand, the event-driven method attracts attention the moment something happens, so it can be dealt with immediately. However, there is the possibility that a fresh event may occur whilst the previous one is being dealt with. In embedded systems, this requires some sort of priority scheme to be attached to different events. As an example, in a video-recorder, reaching the end of the tape when rewinding is an event that needs a high priority because failure to deal with it promptly may well result in the tape being broken. Assigning such priorities is an important part of designing embedded systems, but the details are beyond the scope of this course.

4.2 Non-embedded systems

Whenever you sit using your computer, at least one program is running (its instructions are being obeyed). What you see on the screen is put there by a program; what you type at the keyboard is received by a program; mouse clicks or movements are dealt with by a program. In fact, there are several layers of programs between you (the user) and the hardware of the machine. Collectively, the programs that make the computer able to use word-processing or other programs are called the **operating system**. It is the responsibility of the operating system (OS for short) to act as a combination of housekeeper to organise the hardware, referee to decide conflicting claims on the computer's facilities, and protector to stop programs or users doing things that might damage the hardware or other software. Programs which the user chooses to work with, such as spreadsheet or word-processing programs, are usually referred to as **application programs**.

Both as a computer user and as a writer of programs, most of the time there is very little that you need to know about the detail of the operating system. An overall view of the basic ideas is quite sufficient. The main ideas are illustrated in the following example.

Example 4.1 Using a word-processor

The diagram below shows the main window of a word-processing program.

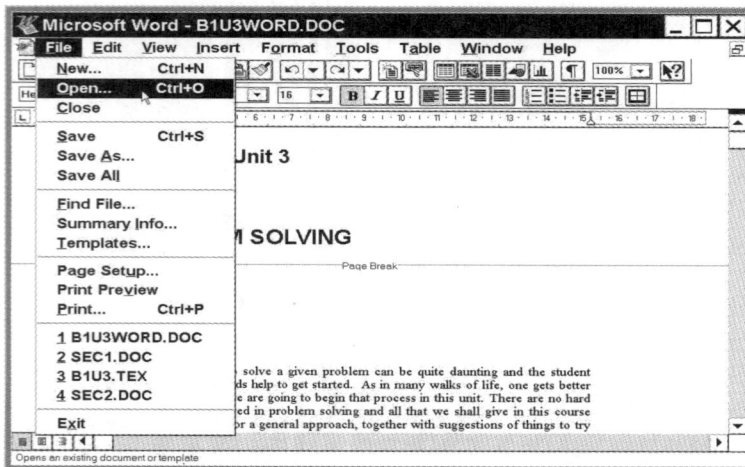

What happens when the user moves the mouse pointer to the `File|Open...` menu item provided by the word-processing program, and clicks the left mouse button? The sequence of events is actually quite complicated. The following diagram illustrates in general the relationship between the word-processing program, the operating system, the hardware and input and output devices. The numbers 1–5 on that diagram represent a five-step approximation to the actual sequence. Each step is described below. (The arrows without numbers in the diagram represent events that are not used in this example.)

word-processing program

4 ↑   5 ↓

operating system (Windows)

1 ↑   2,5 ↓   3 ↑

computer hardware

1 ↑   2,5 ↓

keyboard	mouse	screen	printer

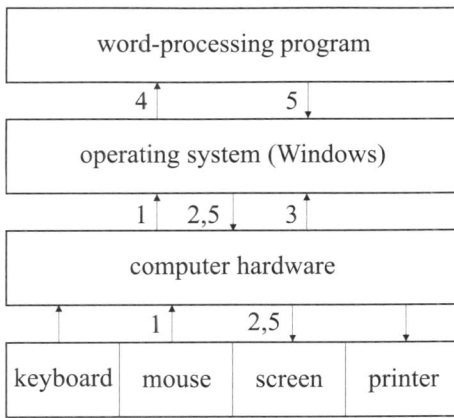

The five steps are as follows.

1. The movement of the mouse generates information that the hardware passes to the operating system.

2. The operating system calculates where the mouse pointer should appear on the screen and instructs the hardware to draw it in the correct position.

3. The mouse button click generates information that the hardware passes to the operating system. The operating system knows where it previously drew the menu item and the mouse pointer, so it knows that the `File|Open...` menu item in the word-processing program window has been 'pressed'.

4. The operating system informs the word-processing program that the `File|Open...` menu item has been chosen, and asks the program to deal with it.

5. The word-processing program makes a series of requests to the operating system that result in the user being asked for a file name and the file being opened.

Although the user appears to be interacting with the word-processing program, the interaction goes through at least two intermediate stages, the hardware and the operating system. Some user actions (for example, moving the mouse) often do not result in *any* action by the program — it is all done by the operating system and hardware. □

Throughout this course, the issue of how user actions cause information to be passed from the hardware to the operating system is ignored. It will be assumed that the operating system 'knows' where the mouse is, which keyboard keys are pressed and so on. It will be assumed that our programs have to respond to messages from the operating system about what the user has done, and send messages to the operating system to be passed on to the user (via the screen, etc.). To summarise in this model of writing programs, it is assumed that the user *does* interact with the program, rather than the hardware.

The description of the interaction between user, computer and operating system in the example above applies to most modern operating systems. When approaches to writing programs are considered, it is useful to split the operating system into two parts: the part that provides services to programs, and the part that provides an interface to the user. The split is not totally satisfactory, but does help in some ways.

The service part of the operating system does the housekeeping and refereeing activities mentioned earlier. The user interface part is concerned with what the user sees on screen and dealing with user activities such as mouse movements and clicks, keypresses, and so on.

The design of user interfaces is a complex area since it has to deal with psychological issues as well as purely technical computing ones. This course cannot discuss such matters, important though they are, but they are tackled in some of the other Open University computing courses. The user interface provided by the *Windows* operating system specified for studying this course is available and will be used. Even if the latest HCI research says otherwise, the `File` menu should appear at the left-hand side of the menu bar (if your program needs a file menu). That is where *Windows* users have come to expect the `File` menu to be; do otherwise, and you will confuse them so that they will not buy your program!

There is much active research in this area (usually known as 'human–computer interaction', or HCI).

In spite of this pragmatic approach, much of what we do is equally applicable to (say) a computer running the *Unix* operating system with the *X-Windows* user interface.

If you have been in computing for a long time (or know people who have), you will be aware that user interfaces for personal computers used to be much more primitive. The user could type commands at the keyboard (no mouse), and the computer could respond with text on the screen or on a printer. In such an environment, one program would be running at a time (apart from the operating system), and the *program* would be in control: it would prompt the user when input was required, and would produce output when it wanted to. The programmer was in control of the whole process, and the procedural programming model was normally used. Even with operating systems, such as *Unix*, which permit several programs to run simultaneously, the program(s) still controlled the user, rather than the other way round.

Contrast this with the *Windows* environment. When working with the *Windows* operating system, the user may have a number of program windows open on the screen. The user can ignore one program for a while and work with another. A program usually does nothing (visibly, at least) until the user prods it into action. The program is supposed to respond to things that the user does, and what the user does cannot be controlled when the program is being written. Thus the event-driven model is appropriate for such an environment. Within a *Windows* program, there are sometimes parts that will not allow the user much choice. For example, some dialog boxes will not permit the user to do anything else until the box has been closed. Thus, briefly, the program is in total control of the user.

The code that is written to make a program respond to events shares many basic principles with code for procedural programs. There is also a huge number of procedural programs that have to be maintained. For these reasons, and because it is slightly easier to learn the basic principles with procedural programs, that is how you are going to start. The first two blocks of this course will tackle fundamental programming ideas in a way that ignores most of the features of *Windows*. We concentrate on the analysis of problems and design of solutions which are then implemented as procedural programs. In the final two blocks, we revisit some of these problems (and investigate many new ones) to see how the analysis and design of solutions can be modified so that the resulting programs look like 'proper' *Windows* programs.

Starting in this way avoids getting involved with code demanded by the operating system that may obscure the principles.

Alongside the change from procedural to event-driven programming, there has been another important development. A number of programming tasks are needed by many programs. A simple example is that almost all

Windows programs offer a `File` menu with an `Open` option. To have to rewrite the code to handle opening files for every separate program is clearly silly. The task should be done once, in such a way that the code can be re-used and incorporated in any program that needs it.

The development of re-usable code is not restricted to event-driven programming; you will be provided with re-usable blocks of code in the early part of the course. Indeed, the early development of operating systems was driven by the need to save programmers from having to deal with low-level details of hardware every time that they wrote a program. However, the complexity of programming dialog boxes, windows, and so on, has greatly encouraged the trend.

The move towards writing re-usable code has had other effects. If a programmer is to make use of a section of code written by someone else, then exactly *what* the code does has to be quite clear. *How* the code does it is totally unimportant to the person using it. The programmer needs to know, for example, what information has to be supplied, what information is returned, and what the relationship between the two is. A typical dialog box for opening a file, for example, is given a file specification which says what types of file the user is allowed to choose from, and it returns the name of the file chosen by the user. Just how the dialog box achieves its purpose the programmer need not worry about.

The description of *what* a piece of code does is called its **specification**; *how* it achieves its purpose is called its **implementation**. The distinction between specification and implementation is important and will receive some attention in this course. To make it possible for you to begin writing programs, you are provided with some re-usable code. You are also given the specification for each piece of re-usable code, to enable you to use that piece. Later in the course, in Blocks III and IV, you will be making extensive use of the re-usable code in the toolkit provided by the course software.

The importance of distinguishing between specification and implementation goes beyond re-using code; in any programming project involving more than one programmer, there is the same need to have specifications of what each team member's code is to do, with the implementation being up to the individual. The C++ language provides a way of separating specifications from implementation. Each section of a project has a **header file** and a **code file**. The header file is only *required* to contain the syntax (format) for using the facilities provided by the corresponding code file. The course team would suggest that it *should* contain sufficient comments to turn it into a specification. The code file contains the C++ code for the implementation. The files are identified by a naming convention: header file names always end in `.h`, and code files always end in `.cpp` (derived from C++).

For the libraries supplied with Builder, only the header files are readable. The code files have been compiled and are supplied in a form that can be incorporated into a program but which is not human-readable. (The incorporation is done when the compiler progress dialog box shows that 'linking' is happening.)

Both the availability of re-usable code toolkits and the practice of project management have encouraged the idea that programmers should develop code in small, independent 'modules', each with a proper specification. Small modules are easier to test and maintain. Where appropriate, you will be encouraged to write your programs as a number of separate modules so that you can test them a small piece at a time.

A few words about programs themselves bring this section to a close. As mentioned earlier, ultimately everything inside a computer is an electronic representation of 0s and 1s. Thus instructions to the processor must consist of binary patterns, usually called **machine code**. Fortunately, the operating system allows us to work with characters on a keyboard and a mouse for input, and with words and pictures on a screen or printer for output.

For embedded computers, the language used to write programs is often very close to the actual machine code. Such languages require little translation, and are often more efficient in their use of storage space and processor time, both of which may be at a premium in embedded computers. However, they also require detailed knowledge of the internal workings of the computer and are difficult to read and maintain. These languages are referred to as 'low-level' ones because they are very close to machine code.

Increasingly, languages such as C^{++} are being used for such programming tasks, but the need for detailed knowledge of the internals has not gone away because of the very limited resources that such embedded systems offer.

Our programs will be written in a high-level language, C^{++}, that bears some resemblance to ordinary language, though used more precisely, and will be translated into the machine code that the computer can actually use by part of the Builder software. There is a wide choice of such high-level languages available, each with its own particular merits.

Even if you need to work with a language different from C^{++}, you should find applying the MT262 ideas fairly straightforward as most high-level languages have much in common.

It is nearly impossible to write the first draft of a program of more than 10–20 lines and make no errors. You may write things which are not acceptable as C^{++}. In this case Builder will tell you when it tries to compile your program.

Your program may compile and run but produce incorrect results. This situation may be caused by a faulty design or faulty coding of the design or, even more likely, by the user doing something that you had not foreseen. Unfortunately, Builder cannot tell you directly about the cause of such errors, although it does provide tools to help track down problems. The types of errors that can arise and some methods of tracking them down are discussed in *Unit 4* of this block.

The following example illustrates, in one case, the size of the problem caused by unexpected actions of users. The software used to typeset the text you are reading contains some ten thousand lines of code similar to the code that you will be writing. Of this, less than one-third deals with the typesetting itself; the rest is for detecting and recovering from various possible error conditions caused by the user. There is some evidence that this proportion of one-third of effort on doing the intended job to two-thirds anticipating errors is reasonable for large programs. (Smaller programs often need to devote a greater proportion to dealing with errors.) If programs devote less than this amount of effort to dealing with errors, then they are probably missing something! Having said that, the early programming exercises will accept some risk of errors due to unexpected user actions so that the error-trapping part of the program does not obscure the rest.

5 Computer hardware

Because any specific statements about hardware are likely to be out of date before this text is printed, only general principles are mentioned here. Although absolute costs change dramatically month by month, usually downwards, *relative* costs of different items have remained fairly constant.

It used to be traditional to separate computers into different categories: large systems called **mainframes**, intermediate systems called **minicomputers**, small systems or **micros**, and **embedded** systems. This division is much less helpful than it used to be, mostly because the boundaries are now very blurred. The only division that has really survived is the one between embedded computers, that normally tackle one specific task, and the rest. Even quite modest personal computers can carry out several tasks (apparently) simultaneously, and cope with several users if suitably equipped. Trying to categorise computers is made even harder by the growing tendency for computers to be connected to a network in which some tasks (printing, for example) may be shared with other computers connected to the network. No division beyond embedded systems and the rest will be made in MT262. Common features will be the focus of our interest.

In order to do useful work, a computer must have the following features.
1. The ability to receive information from the world outside itself — **input**.
2. The ability to give information to the world outside itself — **output**.
3. The facility to store the program(s) that it is currently using.
4. The ability to process information.
5. The facility to store information internally for 'working' or intermediate results.

The information in items 1 and 2 may flow between the computer and humans or between the computer and other computers.

Input devices that might be used include:
o   keyboard,
o   mouse,
o   scanner,
o   microphone,
o   camera (still or video),
o   cable linking to other computers (network),
o   modem linking to a telephone line,
o   bar-code reader (much used for pricing goods),
o   card-reader (used for bank cash machines, etc.).

Output devices include:
o   monitor screen,
o   printer,
o   plotter,
o   loudspeakers driven by a sound card,
o   cable linking to other computers (network),
o   modem linking to a telephone line,
o   an industrial machine tool.

Storage is considered next. In practice, the same facilities are used for program storage and working storage. For most internal working storage (programs and information), some electronic devices are provided that give very high speed access to the stored information. This is referred to as **RAM**, standing for **R**andom **A**ccess **M**emory. The term random access means that any piece of stored information can be retrieved without wading through other information. The amount of RAM provided is one important fact about a computer. Electronically, RAM can be thought of as a collection of switches, each on or off. If it is agreed that 'on' will represent the digit 1 and 'off' will represent 0, RAM can be thought of as storing 0s and 1s, or binary digits (bits for short). Ultimately, all information in and around computers is represented by electronic versions of patterns of 0s and 1s. For historical reasons, a group of 8 binary digits is called a **byte**, and the amount of RAM in a computer is measured by how many bytes can be stored. This persists, even though information is usually moved around internally at least 4 or 8 bytes at a time. RAM can be written to and read from by the part of the computer that actually manipulates information. The information in RAM normally disappears when the power is switched off, although in embedded microprocessors, there may be some RAM which uses a battery to retain information when the power is switched off.

In the past it was usual to use particular types of storage for particular purposes, but some of the boundaries are becoming rather blurred.

The usual unit for measuring the amount of RAM is the **megabyte** (MB). Although the prefix 'mega' really means one million, because of the way in which information is retrieved from RAM, in computing it often means

The system in which only 0 and 1 are used to represent numbers is called the **binary system**.

$$2^{20} = 1\,048\,576,$$

which is slightly more than 1 million. Although quite modestly-priced PCs may have many megabytes of RAM, embedded systems in some domestic appliances may have only a few hundred bytes.

There is another, extremely important, form of internal storage. When you first switch on your computer, a program executes that tests the main components of the computer and then gets the machine to a state where you can use it. This initial program is permanently stored in what is called **ROM**, standing for **R**ead **O**nly **M**emory. Unlike RAM, ROM retains information even when the power is off, which is why it is used for the initial program.

In a PC, the ROM-based startup program might use $\frac{1}{4}$MB. For an embedded system, the program that enables it to control the video-recorder, or whatever, is stored in ROM and is often the only program that is ever used. Embedded systems provide a wide range of ROM sizes, sometimes as large as on a PC.

The next level of storage, magnetic disk, combines the virtues of RAM and ROM. It can be written to as well as read, and retains the information when power is switched off. The penalty paid for these combined virtues is that access to the information is slower than to RAM; typically, it takes 1000 to 10 000 times longer to retrieve a byte from such a disk than from RAM. In compensation, the cost per megabyte is typically one-fiftieth of the cost of RAM. Like RAM, all pieces of data can be accessed (almost) equally easily. Magnetic disks are not often provided for embedded systems, although printers are something of a special case and do sometimes have such storage attached.

For large-scale storage in *personal* computers, **hard disks** are used. These are rigid ('hard') disks coated in magnetic particles which spin in a sealed case. The information is stored by magnetising the particles in one of two directions, representing 0 and 1. The disks, the motor for spinning the disks, and the electronics for reading and writing the information usually form a sealed unit. At the time of writing, a hard disk assembly measuring 100 mm by 150 mm by 20 mm can provide storage of anything from 1000 megabytes to 75 000 megabytes (75 gigabytes). In 10 years, the capacity of hard disks has gone up by a factor of 100, and the price per megabyte has reduced by a factor of 100. There is every reason to suppose that this trend will continue.

<aside>1 gigabyte is 1000 (or sometimes 1024) megabytes.</aside>

Usually, hard disks are bolted into the computer with which they are used. However, versions that can be transferred from machine to machine are increasingly popular. Such 'removable' hard disks provide an easy way to transport large quantities of information between computers. Some of these removable hard disk systems involve removing the whole disk and electronics unit; others have a disk assembly that can be removed from the motor and electronics unit. Some care is needed in either case as both systems are physically somewhat fragile.

For small-scale transfer between personal computers, **floppy disks** are used. These consist of a flexible ('floppy') disk made of plastic film, coated with magnetic particles and enclosed in a rigid plastic casing for protection. The motor and electronic assembly is permanently mounted in the computer, but the disks can be removed and replaced easily. Floppy disks are more likely to survive being mailed than is a removable hard disk system. However, the storage capacity of floppy disks is not large, a few megabytes at most, and the cost per megabyte is actually higher than for hard disks. Moreover, they are slower to access than hard disks. In spite of the snags, floppy disks are still (at the time of writing) a popular choice for taking small quantites of data from one computer to another.

Any form of magnetic storage where the disk can be separated from the electronics doing the recording and replay suffers from one real problem. They are all susceptible to damage from magnetic fields, dust, spilled drinks, pet hairs and smoke. Where danger from such things exists, considerable care should be taken with disks, and the devices that use the disks may need regular cleaning.

There is a form of disk storage that corresponds to ROM, the **CD-ROM**. These do not use magnetism for storage, and are physically more robust than either hard or floppy disks. They have storage capacity comparable with smaller hard disks and cost per megabyte about one-tenth of the price for hard disks. CD-ROMs cannot be used for writing to, but they are a very useful way of distributing large quantities of information cheaply — hence their use for the course software.

<aside>There are also *writable* CDs, these are not strictly CD-ROMs. There are two forms of writable CDs: write once CD-Rs and rewritable CD-RWs. Large capacity DVD-ROMs are also available (read-only) as are DVD-RAMs (rewritable).</aside>

Existing forms of storage are being improved in capacity and cost, on a continuing basis. Some new forms are also being developed. The only reasonable assertion to make is that the cost of storage of all forms is falling steadily, and access speeds and capacities are improving on an almost daily basis.

Finally, there is an important class of storage that is less usually provided on personal computers: tape. Here the storage is on a relative of the magnetic tape used for audio-recording, housed in a distant relative of the audio-cassette. Tape provides a cheap (comparable with CD-ROM), portable way of keeping large quantities of information (up to the capacity of the largest hard disks). Unlike CD-ROM, tapes can be written to as well as read. However, because of the way information is recorded on the tape, it may be necessary to wind on a number of metres of tape to get at a particular byte. Winding tape is a fairly slow process, so tape is not used for information where random access is important. The usual use for tape is to make safety ('back-up') copies of information.

The only safe thing to say about the part of a computer that actually manipulates information, the **processor**, is that processors are getting faster. In 10 years, the speed with which instructions can be carried out by processors in PCs has risen by a factor of about 25–50. Again, this trend looks set to continue although there are signs that the limits of current technology will be reached sometime in the next 10–15 years. On the other hand, in embedded systems, processor types have much longer lives. Some of the processors currently used in embedded systems are designs which are many years old.

The acronym **CPU** that often appears in computer literature is for **C**entral **P**rocessing **U**nit. In the context of PCs, this refers to the main processor, not the others mentioned below.

Embedded systems often have a single processor. However, even a modestly specified personal computer has at least four processors apart from the main one, one for each of the following tasks: handling the screen display, controlling the keyboard, controlling the floppy disk drive(s) and controlling the hard disk drive(s).

This brief discussion of the parts that make up a computer system has left out many interesting topics. It has concentrated on the main areas that will be important for the rest of the course.

Objectives

After working through this unit, you should be able to:

o open Builder by means of the shortcut;

o name each of the windows of Builder's initial screen, and describe the main role of each;

o execute instructions presented in the form

$$(\dots)\mid(\dots)\mid(\dots)\mid(\dots)\dots;$$

o edit existing code, given detailed instructions and advice;

o begin a new project from scratch, given detailed instructions and advice;

o use and understand the use of the following terms: embedded system, procedural model of programming, event-driven model of programming, source, compile, debug, programming environment, variable, identifier, operating system, application program, code specification, code implementation, input, output, bit, byte, megabyte, RAM, ROM.

The level of understanding of the various terms is expected to be the same as that used in the unit. Many of the concepts will be revisited to extend your understanding of them.

You are *not* expected to have mastered the Builder facilities to which you have been exposed. They will all be revisited in later units.

Appendix: Software issues

Windows issues

Windows is a complex operating system which can be changed to suit the preferences of the user. At the time of writing, *Windows 98/ME* (the 'domestic' versions) and *Windows 2000* (the 'office' version) are distinct and differ in a few details of appearance. The declared intention of Microsoft is that the two versions will converge in future. These facts mean that a number of details of the appearance of program windows may not be as illustrated in the text. The most important areas where differences may be noticeable are listed here.

o   Relative positions of windows on the screen may vary.

o   DOS box windows (command prompt windows) may have a toolbar as well as a title bar.

o   The extension part of file names may or may not appear in `File|Open...` and `File|Save` dialog boxes.

o   The layout of dialog boxes may vary; this is likely to occur only with major new versions of *Windows*.

o   The drive letter corresponding to your CD-ROM drive is *very* likely to be different from other people's.

o   The precise default location for the Builder installation *may* change when a major new version of *Windows* is released.

o   The precise name of the icon on which you click to explore the folders and files on your system may be different from the current standard `My Computer`. Differences here may be caused by new versions or by changing preferences.

The software can be judged to be correctly installed if the *contents* of windows and the *general* appearance are as have been described in the text. It is strongly recommended that you make file 'extensions' visible. The different versions of *Windows* offer different ways of doing this, please consult *Windows* Help to find out how to do this.

Common mistakes

The course material was tested by people who were chosen as being fairly inexperienced *Windows* users, and some common errors emerged. These errors are indicated below.

o Using `File|Save` or `File|Save As...` for the initial save of a new project, instead of the correct `File|Save Project As...`. This can lead to some extremely puzzling subsequent errors when you try to run the project.

o Using `File|Open...` to open a project supplied by the course team instead of the correct `File|Open Project...`. This apparently succeeds, but an attempt to run the new project may either fail completely or result in the *previous* project being run. This can be extremely confusing. It may also work correctly.

o Adding `MT262io.lib` to a console application project but failing to add the `#include "MT262io.h"` line to the code file. This gives 'undefined...' compiler errors.

o Doing the reverse of the previous mistake. This leads to linker errors.

o Typing `#include "MT262io.lib"` instead of `#include "MT262io.h"` causes the brief appearance of an incomprehensible error message and the corruption of the library file, causing linker errors. Use *Windows* Explorer to copy an uncorrupted version of the library file from the library archives folder to your working folder.

o Closing the Code Editor window when the intention was to close Builder itself. (The table under 'Unexpected happenings' below explains how to recover from this.)

Before using a lot of time chasing errors in your program code, you should run through the list above to make sure that you have not made one of the errors in the list. It is always wise to inspect the title bar of Builder, because it shows what project Builder is going to run when asked. As indicated above, that may not be quite what you wanted. Then you should check the labels on any tabs in the Code Editor window; these show the files being edited. The title bar of the Code Editor window also shows the file currently being worked on.

Useful shortcuts

Many of the most commonly used menu items have buttons ('speed buttons') provided as alternatives. The buttons appear on the main Builder window in the Toolbar, to the left of the tabbed area (the Component Palette). If these areas are not visible, choose View|Toolbar and make sure all the named toolbars on the flyout menu are checked. Leaving the mouse pointer over a button for a few seconds (without clicking) produces a clue as to what the button is for. As a further complication, some also have keyboard shortcuts. The following table lists a few of the most useful ones; you may wish to add to this any that you find particularly useful.

Menu item	Button	Keyboard
Run|Run Compile without running	Green triangle ('play' symbol)	F9 Ctrl+F9
Project|Add to Project...	File with green + sign	Shift+F11

File|Save	Floppy disk icon
	    Do not use this by mistake when
	    you should use File|Save Project As...
		Ctrl+S

File|Save all	Pile of documents, just to right of floppy disk icon	Shift+Ctrl+S

Disk space

The default installation of Builder is arranged so that project work is as fast as possible. Unfortunately, this means that each project generates some ancillary files which can take up quite a lot of disk space. (It may reach 5 MB per project or more.) If you have made any changes to Builder's options other than those specified in Section 3, then even more files may be generated. If your system starts giving messages indicating that you are short of disk space, then you can reclaim disk space in two ways.

The first way reclaims space from old projects, but does not prevent the creation of the ancillary files for current projects.

○ Open *Windows* Explorer by right-clicking on the My Computer icon and choosing Explore.

○ Choose Tools|Find|Files or Folders....

○ In the Named box, enter *.il?,*.tds.

○ In the Look in box, enter C:\MT262 and make sure that the Include subfolders box has a check mark.

○ Choose Find Now.

○ When the search finishes, highlight all the files found, and delete them by pressing the Delete key. (The files found, which have extensions .ilc, .ils, .tds, etc., are generated at compile-time, and are no longer needed.)

○ Empty the Recycle Bin.

This should recover quite a lot of disk space.

Unless you are very short of disk space, using the above method of deleting files from time to time should suffice. The second way requires that you set an option in Builder, but do delete the files as described above first.

o   Start Builder, and choose `Project|Options...` from the main menu.
o   Choose the `Linker` tab, and make sure that the
    `Don't generate state files` box is checked.
o   Choose `OK`.

These actions reset the project options to the default, so they will be needed only if you have changed anything in `Project|Options...`.

There is no way of preventing the `.tds` files from being created if the ability to debug programs is to be retained. Removing such files from time to time is harmless, since the one for the current project will be re-created the next time the project is compiled or run.

Unexpected happenings

Many of the unexpected things that may happen when you use Builder are covered above. The following table lists the commonest ones and ways to recover quickly. It also lists some of the most common errors that can appear when you try to run your program, and the most likely causes.

Symptom	Suggested action and/or cause
Code Editor window disappears	1. `View|Units` or press `Ctrl+F12`
	and double-click on the file that you want to edit
Code Editor window covered by a 'form'	press `F12`
Object Inspector window disappears	`View|Object Inspector` or press `F11`
Form disappears	`View|Forms` and double-click on the form that you want to view
Error message 'statement missing ;'	Insert semicolon at end of line *before* highlighted one
Error message 'undefined...'	1. Misspelt identifier: check upper- and lower-case letters
	2. Missing header file: ensure that any `#include` statements are as specified in the text
Linker error 'undefined...'	File not added correctly to project
	Use `Project|Add to Project...`
Mysterious compiling errors with a new 'Console Application'	Make sure that the check box marked `Use VCL` was checked in the `Console Wizard`. If this is not done errors may be reported in a file which seems to be nothing to do with your project. The only safe way to recover is to start again allowing files from your first attempt to be overwritten.

Solutions to the Computer Activities

Section 3

Solution 3.1

(a) The title bar of Builder shows `C++Builder5 - Project1`. Project1 is the default name for a programming project that you have not yet named.

(b) The title bar now shows the name you gave the project:
`C++Builder - Hello1`

(c) What *should* happen is that a dialog box should appear with messages about 'compiling' and then 'linking'. When the dialog box disappears, Builder will minimise and a window like the following should open. It is referred to as the **program window**.

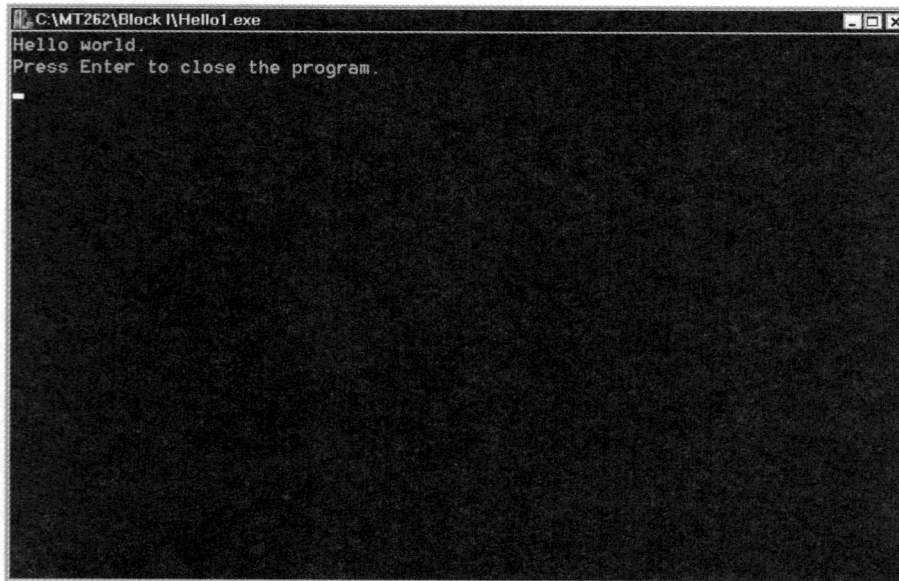

What *may* happen is that the Code Editor window may acquire a highlighted line and a message at the bottom about error(s). If this happens, please check very carefully that the code you entered in this part of the activity is exactly as shown, with all spelling correct and all punctuation in place.

(If you were to press the Enter key, the new window would vanish and Builder would reappear.)

(d) The dialog box with 'compiling' and 'linking' messages will reappear but, when it closes, the window with the 'Hello world.' message will appear only briefly.

Solution 3.2

Each statement of the form `puts("...")` causes whatever is between the quotation marks to be written on the screen.

Solution 3.3

(a) There should be three messages in the window.

```
[C++ Error] VATU.cpp(21): E2268 Call to undefined function 'WriteString'.
[C++ Error] VATU.cpp(22): E2268 Call to undefined function 'WriteFloat'.
[C++ Error] VATU.cpp(24): E2268 Call to undefined function 'getchar'.
```

The numbers in the parentheses after VAT.cpp are the line number locations of the errors in the code. (Your line numbers may differ slightly from those given here.) Each line of code, each comment and each blank line is counted. (If there are any other messages, check the spelling of all code carefully, including the placing of semicolons, and make any necessary corrections.)

(b) The changes should have removed the error messages, and the program should run. If not, check that you made both the changes described.

Solution 3.4

(a) The heading of 'Form1' has changed to 'Hello'.

(b) The compiler progress dialog box appears with the 'compiling' and 'linking' messages in turn. You may find that this process takes rather longer than for the first program. Eventually, Builder will minimise and a window will appear with the caption 'Hello'. It can be closed either by clicking on the cross icon or by double-clicking on the top left-hand corner icon.

(c) The box near the top of the Object Inspector says Button1: TButton and the Caption entry reflects what appears on the button itself, namely Button1.

(d) Compiling should be a little faster this time. The program window should appear, complete with caption and the new button, but clicking on the button achieves nothing.

(e) (i) You should be switched to the Code Editor window in the middle of a skeleton section of code looking like the following.

```
//----------------------------------------------------------
void __fastcall TForm1::Button1Click(TObject *Sender)
{

}
//----------------------------------------------------------
```

(ii) Provided that there were no errors during compiling, the button should now close the program window.

(iii) The OnClick entry is no longer blank, as the others are. It refers to Button1Click, which you may also have observed appears in the code skeleton that Builder created and in which you placed the Close(); line.

Solution 3.5

No solutions are provided because you were not asked any questions.

Index